Sometimes You Need a 2X4

Practices, Tactics, Creative Ideas and Knowledge That
Make Highly Successful Sales Professionals Great
(Stuff They Likely Didn't Cover in Your Sales Training)

By Tim Kedzuch

Contents

What's in it for you?

Simply put...greater sales success.

There are several practices, creative ideas and characteristics that have been learned by or are intuitive to top performing sales professionals which are the foundation of their extraordinary success. Unfortunately, these ideas and practices are often overlooked during sales training but are the pillars on which you can increase your sales successes and enhance your career. They are the fundamental habits, tactics, ideas and traits which separate the great salesperson from the good and the good from the average. People often think that top performing salespeople are born great not made. Reality shows, however, that good sales professionals can be great if they are perceptive enough to recognize and apply ideas and techniques learned from highly successful sales professionals as well as their own positive experiences.

During my 40 years in sales, I've been fortunate to know and learn from a number of high energy, extremely successful professionals who helped fine tune my sales techniques, enhanced my skills and inspired me to reach for the stars. Additionally, carefully listening to prospects and customers sparked valuable creative ideas which also elevated my game.

The following pages contain a compilation of the principles, knowledge and practices found in extraordinarily successful sales professionals. They come from numerous brilliant, high producing salespeople I've known as well as my own positive experiences during 40 years of very successful sales.

You've likely heard about the 4 P's of marketing which are product, price, promotion and place. High earning sales professionals know there are 4 P's to sales as well – passion, perception, performance and perseverance which are the underlying theme throughout this book. Whether you're a seasoned sales veteran or just starting your sales adventure, you're sure to find ideas in this book which will sharpen your skills and make you a better, more productive sales professional.

Since your time is a precious commodity, this book is purposely short, to the point and a quick read. You will, however, find that it's filled with impactful ideas sure to peak your imagination, challenge your sales senses and help you succeed at a higher level.

By the way, I began writing this book when the world was "normal" but the effects of the coronavirus in 2020 will certainly impact the sales process in the future. Stay at home orders put in place by states, cities and counties have mandated that we currently do business differently. While work from home has caused us to look for new ways to connect with prospects and customers, the ideas and tactics outlined in this book remain valid and extremely useful.

Nothing can replace face-to-face meetings with our prospects and customers as integral components in building relationships and sales. Hopefully, we'll all get back to some sort of normal soon. In the meantime, you can, with a little imagination, adapt these many creative tactics and ideas from highly successful sales professionals to any sort of customer connection.

Good luck and good selling.

"There is no strong performance without a little fanaticism in the performer." – Ralph Waldo Emerson, Essayist, lecturer, philosopher and poet

Fire Within

For any salesperson, whether experienced or beginner, this chapter should be a no-brainer. It deals with the most primal attribute which separates highly productive salespeople from the good and the good from the just plain average. My high school football coach called it "intestinal fortitude." In his book, "The X Factor A Quest for Excellence" George Plimpton called it the "X Factor." It's that basic driving force inside which makes great salespeople want to get up in the morning and look forward to spreading the word about their product, service or cause.

High performing sales professionals all have a deeply rooted passion to succeed for themselves, their company and, most importantly, their customers. Passion may be present in everyone's DNA but, in high achieving salespeople, it creates a fire within which drives them to focus attention on all the details necessary to grow professionally, to excel and work at 110% all the time. Passion provides them with a sense of invincibility, strength, perseverance and confidence which leads to increased sales results. It helps top performers develop a sense that their game far exceeds their ability, increases adrenaline and moves them into a zone which carries them through any situation and overcome any obstacles. Passion drives dedication which means they never leave a prospect/customer meeting or conversation wondering what else they could have said or done. Most importantly, visible and recognizable passion creates animated prospect and customer meetings, engages prospects and generates a sense of believability so vital to success. True, sincere passion provides energy and determination to confront problems, find solutions and to motivate others to take action.

What Should You Really be Passionate About?

In sales, passion to win just to satisfy one's ego or just to make more money, however, is not enough to promote and maintain long term sales growth. Everyone has some level of passion about things they believe deeply about personally. Truly successful sales professionals, however, are passionate about providing great, highly satisfying solutions for their prospects and customers. They focus their drive and their presentations on how their product or service will positively affect the person or the company on whom they are calling. When you're sincerely passionate about satisfying your prospects' or customers' needs, you'll capture and hold their attention, energize meetings and create a high level of comfort, trust and confidence...all vital components to building long lasting relationships and sales. Additionally, passionately showing that you care about your prospects' or customer's needs contributes mightily to fending off sales erosion to competitors.

Sure, a quick sale may make your management happy and make you look like a hero. But your long-term success depends on developing an unbreakable bond with your prospects and customers based on the trust and confidence sincere passion will generate.

One of the salespeople who influenced my success over the years was a slight, somewhat unassuming person who, under normal circumstances, was quiet and almost introverted. He was, however, so totally convinced of the value his product represented and the positive affect it had on customers' needs that it elevated his game enormously. His passion was so strong that it transformed him into a different person in front of prospects and customers which created a sense of comfort and confidence in his offering. They loved him and trusted him as a partner which led to long term relationships and repeat sales.

Passion is Contagious

There are many sales situations where the person you can reach is only one of several people involved in the buying process. This is often the case in business to business sales where multiple, often inaccessible influences can impact the outcome. In these instances, it becomes essential to make your immediate contact an evangelist for you, your brand and your product. Your passion can turn your contact into an extension of you...selling your product or service to others with a high level of commitment and energy. When you make your immediate contacts passionate about your solutions and the performance of your product or service, they will become zealous about it and will support your cause.

Ask yourself, in addition to being passionate about exceeding the sales goals assigned to you by management, what customer focused solutions can you get excited about? How will your product or service enhance the lives or positions of the people on whom you call? Being passionate about what's important to your prospects and customers will absolutely carry you to greater heights.

Conversely, if you can't be sincerely passionate about the product or service you're selling, it's time to seriously re-evaluate the product or the company with which you work. You may need to move to a different product line offered by your company, move to another company within your industry or, perhaps, change industries altogether. The bottom line is you need to be true to your customers and to yourself and

11

sincerely believe your product or service will enhance the lives of people you're targeting. It's the only way to grow professionally, feel good about what you do as a salesperson and produce at a high level.

The ideas, tactics and strategies outlined in this book will definitely make you a more productive sales professional but your passion to deliver great solutions for your prospects must be the underlying base in order to truly succeed at a higher level. Again, when you show your prospects and customers you are passionately concerned for their needs, they will embrace you, your product or service and make them comfortable with their buying decision.

"It is not your customer's job to remember you. It is your obligation and responsibility to make sure they don't have the chance to forget you." – Patricia Fripp, Speaker, author, sales presentation skills trainer and speech coach

Communicate, Communicate, Communicate

In the late 1800's, German social scientist Hermann Ebbinghaus conducted extensive research focused on human learning and information retention. Ebbinghaus memorized lists of nonsense three letter words and measured the short and long term retention of the information learned. From his research, he concluded that, over time, there exists a forgetting curve through which recall can be measured. Overall, his research showed that people tend to forget approximately 50% of what they learned over 24 hours and as much as 90% of the learned information after 30 days. He also found, however, that repeated learning of or exposure to the information reduced the deterioration in recall and enhanced the level of information retained over the long term.

Given the enormous amount of information delivered to us through a proliferation of media channels today, these research conclusions are likely more on target now than in the late 1800's. Although our overall capacity to learn and retain information is substantial, conscious recall of learned information is directly affected by the constant flow of news, facts and ideas. As people continuously absorb new information, the previously learned information, in both detail and in aggregate grows somewhat vague.

From a sales perspective, this means the information – the benefits, the value, the return on investment, the competitive edge – we provide in presentations whether face-to-face, virtual or by phone begins to fade as soon as the meeting ends. Yet, it's this very information which may be critical in getting or losing the sale when the prospect is ready to buy. In order to ensure continuous top of mind awareness for products and/or services, highly successful sales professionals combine both direct personal contact with indirect communication methods to generate communication booster shots to keep their sales message, image and brand embedded in prospects' minds.

Advertising and marketing professionals clearly understand these basic principles. They recognize that continuity and consistency are the foundations on which to build product and/or service share of mind, preference, demand and ultimately sales. They strategically integrate a variety of media including advertising, trade shows, direct mail, e-mail blasts, websites, social media and other tools to present a consistent and cohesive sales message to prospects and customers. When a prospect or customer is ready to buy, top of mind awareness plays an enormous role in the decision-making process. The more often salespeople make contact in some form, the greater the likelihood their product or service will be included in consideration and ultimately purchased. Consistent exposure to a salesperson and his or her sales message truly is a primary contributor to sales success.

Blending Sales and Marketing Techniques

While many businesspeople tend to think of sales and marketing as separate functions, highly successful sales professionals understand that these disciplines are inseparable partners in their growth. Although their job function may be sales, great sales professionals also think like marketing people.

14

The frequency of personal sales calls and the buying patterns unique to your business will, naturally, dictate the timing for your indirect communications effort as well as the type of media which will work most effectively. What's most important is that you keep in regular contact with your prospects and customers, in some form, to insure top of mind awareness. Although you can't be in front of your prospects and customers constantly, you can reinforce your share of mind by simply planning a consistent program of indirect contact. This regular mix of contact whether by phone, mail, e-mail, text or social media will keep your name, company and product or service fresh in the minds of prospects when they're ready to buy.

One of my customers helped me to learn this valuable lesson early in my career as a business-to-business magazine advertising space salesman. During a meeting with one of the largest advertisers in our market, I asked their communications manager in a tongue-in-cheek way "other than me, who's the best advertising space salesperson who calls on your company?" Her response was fast and direct. She said, "that's easy – it's John" who worked for one of the architectural magazines at the time. The communications manager went on to explain that John regularly sent her information about the market, industry trends, technology, special opportunities and more on a regular basis. She added that some of the information was extremely useful while some simply interesting.

This regular program of communications gave John the opportunity to position himself as a valuable resource to both the communications manager and others within the company...a resource they turned to on a regular basis for information and ideas. At the same time, John's monthly notes, letters or phone calls continued to reinforce awareness for himself and his magazine which helped insure repeat sales. Interestingly, the communications manager said she really couldn't remember how often John actually called on her in person. She said, "it just seemed as though he was there all the time...ready to help."

Top sales achievers, like John, employ a variety of media to assure continuous recognition for their companies, their products and themselves. They strategically balance personal sales calls with indirect communications to consistently position themselves and their companies as invaluable partners concerned with helping their customers satisfy their needs, succeed and prosper. Their regular communications efforts plant seeds for new customer sales growth while defending their existing customer base against sales erosion to competitors. This type of consistent communications effort doesn't require a huge dollar investment or a lot of time. It simply requires an organized database, some creative thinking and discipline.

Content

The contact you make can range from a simple phone call to say "hi" to formal written communications. The information you provide prospects and customers should be brief but interesting and timely. It is intended to cement and/or build your relationship as someone who sincerely cares...someone they should turn to when the time is right to buy. The content will, naturally, depend on the type of business you're in and the needs of the people on whom you call. It can consist of special offers, product developments, industry trends, economic news or other facts which will help consumers/buyers make comfortable, more intelligent buying decisions. You can tap sources within your own company like the marketing department, product development people and research to provide timely information of interest. You can also gather information from outside sources such as the department of commerce, magazine/newspaper articles, websites and trade associations. When sharing this information with others, be sure to credit the source. Doing so provides you with greater credibility and positions you as a valuable resource. Make notes of any information you see, read or hear about your industry which you believe will be of interest to your prospects and customers. You'll be surprised how easy it is to build a file of useful facts to share.

The content you provide should be simple but meaningful and informative. For example, top real estate salespeople send regular mailings to homeowners with information like the selling prices for homes in target clients' neighborhoods. This is public information which is easily accessible. The real estate salesperson often also provides a brief listing of their own sales track records in the area as well as general information about interest rates and other related items. These tend to be passive notes intended to ensure that prospects know their names when it's time to sell or buy a house. They also often include their photograph which adds to the comfort level of prospects and plants a visual impression in their minds. While there are likely many real estate salespeople serving the given target area, the ones who come to mind first are those who keep potential clients informed and constantly build share of mind.

Knowledge Adds Value

In addition to using the content to reinforce your share of mind, the information you provide in an indirect communications program adds perceived value to you, your company and your product. This can be particularly important when you're working in a highly competitive industry and/or when your competition focuses their sales efforts on price. It helps to separate you from the competition and establishes you and your product as something more than a commodity. As a result, it's very important to be serious about the information gathering process.

The Package

Your indirect contact with prospects and customers can be sent in the form of handwritten notes, postcards, letters, e-mail messages and brief messages on the phone. Additionally, media like LinkedIn, Instagram and Twitter provide excellent platforms for outreach once you've established connections and a following. The resource you find most effective will depend on your budget, comfort level and the uniqueness of your business.

For example, a giftware rep with whom I've consulted organized her customer/prospect database by the types of products which sell well in each store. Whenever one of the manufacturers she represents introduces a new product collection, she sends an e-mail blast with attached images of the new introductions to the appropriate group as an integral part of her indirect contact program. She also posts images and a brief statement via her social media accounts to expand her coverage. Her intent with these e-mail blasts and her social media effort is to maintain awareness between personal visits and presented simply as an informational message. This often opens the door to appointments and continues to build on her share of mind. In some cases, it even generates over the phone orders initiated by the retailer.

She uses postcards to invite her entire customer/prospect database to each of the giftware shows in her area. This helps to insure they will at least consider visiting her company's showroom and provides a bit of an edge when competing with hundreds of other showrooms for attendee time. Additionally, she sends a brief handwritten "thank you" note after getting every order whether generated in person, by e-mail or over the phone. This is one additional opportunity to etch her name in the minds of her customers and solidify her relationship with them. Overall, she finds that using a mix of indirect communications media quite effective and makes it more likely her messages will be opened and read.

Another great example comes from a young, talented advertising space salesperson with whom I worked. Every month he created a simple one-page newsletter from the business software installed in his company laptop. He included industry and relevant economic news he gathered, a few cute jokes and a brief message about upcoming issues of his magazine. He sent it to advertisers and prospects as an attachment to an e-mail blast. His simple but informative newsletters became so popular that whenever he didn't send it at the usual time a few regular recipients called thinking they had missed it. He accomplished two very valuable objectives with the program. First, some recipients asked him to add other people at their companies to the newsletter list which provided him with deeper penetration among potential decision makers or influencers. Second, he continued to build confidence and share of mind for himself and his magazine which led directly to continuous growth in sales and share of market.

This all may seem rather simple but it's amazing how many good but potentially great salespeople don't use tools like these to support their direct sales effort. Remember great, highly successful salespeople invest in continuous action to ensure their success. They create a simple but consistent marketing plan to work in concert with their direct sales effort to generated continued sales growth. Share of mind is truly a major contributor to sales success and requires constant nurturing or reinforcement.

*"Skill in the art of communication is crucial to a leader's
success. He can accomplish nothing unless he can
communicate effectively." - Anonymous*

Communication Part 2

Now that we've discussed the importance of consistent
communications to build and maintain share of mind, let's talk
about a few related elements which can have a very positive
affect on the level of your success. Every touch point you have
with your customers and prospects creates an impression in
their minds about you, your trustworthiness, your sincere
concern for them and their goals. This impression is the
springboard to the level of comfort they feel about you as a
partner in their buying process.

Use a Pyramid

The success of any communications with prospects and/or
customers whether in-person, virtual, written or voice mail
depends your ability to capture and maintain their attention
right from the start. Journalists use a pyramid structure when
writing an article which works quite effectively. The first
sentence or paragraph in a story provides a brief overview
intended to capture the interest of and engage the reader. They
then provide expanded details to support the opening and tell
the whole story.

High performance salespeople use a similar approach
when connecting with prospects and customers. They make a
brief statement of "what's in it for you" right up front to
capture prospect or customer attention and make them want

to concentrate and learn more. Take a few minutes to think about how you open your written communications, the subject lines in emails, voice mail messages and even your face-to-face meetings. Ask yourself "Would this opening statement or comment make me want to learn more? Does it draw me into the conversation?" Everyone is busy and often and easily distracted. The first statement or comment you make can set the tone for just how much attention and interest you're going to get from the people who will have an impact on your sales success.

Loose the Word "I"

Take the word "I" out of your communications as much as possible. Rather than using the phrase "I think you should buy this because…" highly successful sales professionals will say something like "You'll benefit enormously by making this purchase because…" The meaning or intent in each of these phrases may be the same but the delivery makes a huge difference in the way you are perceived. Regardless of how much they trust you or know you, ultimately, your prospects and customers really want to know <u>what's in it for them</u>. They want to feel as though they are making the buying decision for their own reasons not necessarily because you think it's a good idea. Always remember, it's about your customer and/or prospect and what makes them feel you're concerned and interested in providing great solutions for them. This minor adjustment in your delivery will contribute to creating a positive impression in your prospect's mind which will certainly influence your relationship and, ultimately, contribute to your sales success.

What does Your Voice Mail Message tell People?

Another simple but extremely important, often overlooked

element in sales communications is the impression you leave in your voice mail message. Yes, this may seem elementary but as mentioned earlier every touch point you have with prospects and customers forms their perception of you, your brand and your product or service. Listen to your voice mail message and ask yourself "Is this someone I want to do business with?" Does your voice mail message sound enthusiastic, warm, interested and welcoming?

Can you imagine the impression a voice mail message like this creates: "Hi this is_____. Leave a message and I'll return your call at my earliest convenience." Yes, that's an actual voice mail message I heard when calling an associate. This salesperson might have said something like: "Hi this is _____. Your call is important to me so please leave a message and I'll return your call as soon as possible." And, then return that call as soon as possible! This may seem like a minor difference, but it shows your customer or prospect respect and that you are interested in talking with them.

Give Them a Reason to Respond

It seems as though everyone is buried with work these days and voicemail truly has become the bane of every salespersons' existence. Whether calling a prospect to arrange for a meeting or to provide a special offer or to simply determine if they are worth pursuing, give them a reason to respond. Focus your message on a something which will drive their curiosity or interest. Keep the message short and to the point leading with what's in it for them. Give them a reason to want to call you back. Again, this may seem elementary but will reduce your frustration and help you make connections. Before you make your call, think about what your prospect or customer will want to hear that will move them to respond.

Additionally, after leaving a voice mail message, top sales performers frequently follow the message with an email note recapping their message and reiterating the reason the prospect will want to respond. This action provides an opportunity to ask the prospect when the timing would be right to call again showing that the salesperson values the prospect's time. It also shows you are persistent and won't give up until they make the connection.

Timing is Everything

Another vital component in communications is the timing. When you promise to provide additional information or a proposal, it's extremely important to get the information to the prospect or customer quickly while your conversation is still fresh in their minds. Far too often the impact of sales communications is reduced when too much time goes by. Prospect and customer perception of you, which can make or break a sale, depends partly on how quickly you respond to promises or their requests.

All your contact with customers and prospects forms an impression in their minds about you, your company and your sincerity. Regardless of how great your product or service may be, people buy from those who they feel are concerned about their needs. Make sure that all your communications show you're committed to them.

"When was the last time you did something for the first time?"
– John C. Maxwell, Author, speaker and pastor

Sometimes It Takes a 2X4

When I was in college, a marketing professor started a lecture with a story which, on the surface, seemed silly but ultimately resonated with the entire class. It was intended for use among marketing and advertising people but certainly has a an equally strong impact as a sales tool. The story went something like this:

One day farmer Pete was driving his pickup truck along the dirt road which separated his farm from that of his neighbor John. As he was driving, he noticed that John was in the middle of the road pulling on the reigns of a mule. When Pete reached them, he got out of his truck and asked his neighbor what was going on. John explained that he was crossing the road when the mule simply stopped and refused to move. Pete said to John "if I get him to move, will you buy me lunch?" John's response was "absolutely, I've been stuck here for over half an hour and I have things to do." That said, Pete walked to the back of his pickup truck, grabbed a 2X4, smacked the mule up the side of the head and the mule immediately followed him across the road. John just stood there with a stunned look on his face and Pete turned to him and said, "John, the first thing you have to do is get his attention."

OK...obviously, I'm not advocating physical abuse of prospects as a sales practice (although, I've certainly felt like it more than a few times). The truth is that every salesperson will deal with people who stubbornly resist them, their sales message, their products/services or company. They may refuse to grant a meeting, ignore attempts to contact them or simply refuse to accept the salesperson as a resource which might provide better solutions than others. This resistance can be the result of bias toward another salesperson or company, ignorance, misunderstanding, insanely busy schedules or just plain laziness to consider something new or different. Since your sales growth depends heavily on making quality connections with prospects or breaking through obstacles, putting creative sales 2X4's to work for you can certainly go a long way toward continued sales growth.

Extreme Examples that Work at Getting Attention

One of the truly brilliant magazine advertising salespeople with whom I worked was faced with a challenge from an important potential customer which called for extreme action. The communications manager of a large electronics component manufacturer was investing a ton of advertising dollars with Bill's competitors but not with his magazine. Bill didn't have a problem getting meetings but the prospect wouldn't buy advertising in Bill's magazine because, as he put it, "I don't see my competitors advertising in your magazine so it makes me wonder if it's the right place for my ad dollars." It was obvious to Bill that this person really wasn't reviewing his magazine since the vast majority of the prospect's competitors where indeed advertising there regularly.

Clearly, this was a perfect opportunity for using a sales "2X4" to get the prospect's attention and overcome the obstacle. Bill had one of the assistants at the magazine collect copies of all the ad pages placed by the prospect's competition over the prior 12 months. They taped the pages together side by side, rolled them into a tube and sent Bill the package. Bill arranged for a meeting telling his prospect he had some important information to share. When he arrived, Bill taped the first page of the roll to the prospect's office door jam, walked around the office taping the ad pages to the wall and dropped the remaining pages on the prospect's desk. Bill said, "these are the ads from your competitors which were published in our magazine over the past 12 months. They are the advertising sales messages your prospects are seeing regularly. Perhaps you've been too busy to see them." The prospect was stunned and included Bill's magazine in the next advertising campaign.

Another example of using an extreme 2X4 comes from a story I heard about an OEM parts salesperson who was finding it impossible to set a meeting with the purchasing manager at an appliance manufacturing facility. It was a company which represented a huge potential for sales volume. As he drove by the plant one day, he noticed there was a highway billboard next to the entrance to the plant parking lot which wasn't being used at the time. He contacted the billboard company and learned he could rent it for a month. He did so with a brief but to-the-point message to the purchasing manager about the tremendous value he and his company could offer and asked for a meeting. He got the meeting and made them a regular customer. This was a big investment on his part and somewhat risky but well worth the effort over the long run.

Additionally, one of the most productive salespeople I've known found a rather fortuitus way to attract attention of prospects and create a memorable impression. Her first name is Gayle and she found a chocolate retailer named Gayle's Chocolates. When she had difficulty connecting with prospects, she would send them a box of Gayle's Chocolates truffles along with a personal note to ask for a meeting in person or a least via the phone. She also used this tactic when needing to move existing customers to take action, to reinforce her strong relationship with them and thank them for their business.

Not so Extreme 2X4's

Extreme measures are not always necessary. There are times when you simply need to cut through the clutter. For example, instead of sending an e-mail to a prospect you're chasing, you might send a message via a snail mail card or letter, a FedEx package or perhaps even a telegram. You might also create and embed a video message in an email or text message. This can be a little time consuming but is a truly dynamic, impactful way to get attention for you and your message. Instructions for embedding email videos can be found via a number of online sites.

When you do leave a voice mail message which can easily be ignored, it's important to follow it up with an email or handwritten snail mail note with a brief compelling reason why your target should get back to you. The key is to find a creative way to capture the attention of your target using disruptive options. It's amazing how many average salespeople settle on using the same old methods to get through to people and don't understand why prospects aren't responding.

Be creative, do something different and look for unconventional solutions. Yes, there are times when nothing will work but it's worth trying creative 2X4's to move people to action. Ultimately, using creative ways to attract a prospect's attention and elevate their level of interest can provide a great, satisfying return for your investment. Most importantly, sales 2X4's create a lasting impression sure to strengthen share of mind for you and your product or service.

"All our knowledge has its origins in our perceptions."
Leonardo da Vinci

Perception and Reality

Highly successful sales professionals know that words and ideas have a way of being interpreted differently by different people often in a way which can alter their understanding of a product offering and the benefits. Prospect and customer perception is a function of their personalities, molded by their life experiences, the environment, education, biases and, at times, a salesperson's competition. Far too often, inexperienced or weak salespeople assume their prospects think the same way they do and the prospect will automatically interpret statements, comments and ideas as intended by the salesperson. They present product or service features and details and assume the prospect will convert them accurately to the benefit. Unfortunately, these assumptions can frequently lead to misunderstanding and/or lost sales.

Learn How Your Prospects Perceive their Needs and Your Product or Service

As you think about strategy for presenting your product or service to prospects, it's essential that you go into every meeting with questions which will help you learn how they think, what product attributes are important to them and what will satisfy their needs before you dive into a presentation. The answers will provide you with insight into which product features are most important to the prospect so that you focus on what they perceive as vital components of the buying process. The answers will also help you clearly understand how your prospects define their needs so that you can make sure you're both on the same page as you present your message.

For example, one of my associates stumbled on an "A-ha" moment early in her sales career which had a long term, positive impact on her sales volume and growth as a sales professional. She was meeting with the Marketing Communications Manager for a company which was investing many thousands of advertising dollars with competitive magazines but not with the magazine she represented. He and my associate got along well but she failed to move him to invest in her publication. After numerous frustrating meetings with him, she decided it was time for her to start over with a clean slate. She began their next meeting by saying, "Tom, I have a briefcase full of reasons why advertising in my magazine will help you reach the right target audience and grow your business but we somehow haven't agreed. So, let's start over with this question, what are you looking for when selecting magazines in which to invest your ad dollars?" Thankfully, Tom was more than willing to answer the question by telling her what criteria or features were important to him and, most importantly, why he felt the magazine she represented didn't fit his needs.

Two extremely valuable sales lessons came from his response. First, Tom's comments gave my associate a list of buying criteria on which she needed to focus and those features which she could minimize or ignore since they weren't important to the him. Second, she had assumed his perception of the magazine's readers and how they fit his target market was in line with her own perception. Given his response, Tom clearly didn't fully understand who her magazine's subscribers were, the kinds of work they did and the value they represented to him and his company. Armed with this information, she focused the conversation on the criteria important to Tom and provided the evidence that, ultimately, changed his perception of the readers. She was then able to position them as high value targets for his company's advertising and sales effort. Their relationship changed dramatically and Tom and his company became a repeat customer. My associate found this to be an enormously valuable lesson and inserted perception questions at the beginning of every subsequent sales meetings.

The Power of Understanding Your Prospects/Customers

Another example of how truly valuable understanding the way your prospects think comes from a very forward-thinking publishing company for which I worked. Every three to four years, the company hired a research firm to conduct advertiser perception studies for their magazines. The studies were designed to measure how marketing and communications people as well as advertising agency media planners perceived their magazines in relation to others serving the various markets. Additionally, they included questions to identify the criteria the marketing and advertising people used to make media buying decisions in each of the markets. On a broad scale, the responses provided them with an overall picture of how prospects and customers positioned the magazines as solutions to their marketing outreach needs and objectives. Additionally, they found that the list of the selling points they thought were important weren't always perfectly aligned with the criteria key buying influencers deemed important. This knowledge and insight guided them in sales direction and tactics as well as the creation of sales material and sales training. This customer first mentality helped them stay on target with sales strategy, stay in touch with the changing needs of advertisers and positioned them as one of the most successful business to business publishing companies in the industry.

Obviously, you likely don't have the resources to conduct perception research studies among all your prospects on a large scale. Like my associate's story earlier, however, you can achieve the same result by asking questions of each of your potential customers before launching into your sales presentation. What end result is your prospect looking for when considering a product or service like yours? How do they perceive your brand and your product or service in relation to their needs? What criteria is important to them in the buying process? It's absolutely essential to remember that everyone has different ideas and perceptions which can directly impact your sales results. This means you need to go through these steps with every one of your prospects.

Top sales producers recognize that one can't assume anything. They ask questions to establish an understanding of how their prospects think, what they want and what will move them. After establishing what's important to the prospect, top performers organize their presentations to lead with the benefit and use the features which fit the prospects' expressed criteria to show how their product or service will satisfy the prospects' needs. As a result, there's little room for misunderstanding which ultimately leads to immediate as well as long-term sustainable sales success.

Lastly, this question and answer session has the added benefit of showing your prospects and customers that you are focused on them and their needs. This enhances your relationship with them and builds trust so vital in sales success.

"I not only bow to the inevitable; I am fortified by it." –
Thornton Wilder, Playwright and novelist

Beware of Quicksand

If you saw the movie "The Replacements,"* you may
remember a locker room post game meeting which included a
terrific example of how powerful our minds and attitudes can
be in directing our success or allowing failure. After a tough
loss, the coach, asked his replacement players what they feared
the most. His question, naturally, generated many humorous
answers from various players. It was the response from the
quarterback, however, which brought the conversation back
into focus. The quarterback said what he feared most was
"quicksand." His teammates were clearly puzzled so the coach
asked him to explain. The quarterback said that "you can think
that everything seems to be going fine then one thing goes
wrong, then another and another. You try to fight back but the
harder you fight the deeper you sink - until you can't move -
can't breathe - because you're in over your head - like
quicksand."

At some point, every salesperson faces situations which
can be considered "quicksand." Factors they can't control and,
in some cases, factors they can and should control break down
levels of concentration, confidence and ultimately sales.
Changes in economic conditions, evolving customer needs,
strategic or tactical changes made by the competition, changes

The movie The Replacements released August 11, 2000
distributed by Warner Brothers. Director Howard Deutch;
Producer Dylan Sellers; Writer Vince McKewin; Production
Company Bel Air Entertainment.

in their company management and/or management philosophy, internal problems with product quality, distribution and even personal problems can cause losing streaks.

It's inevitable that all salespeople will face challenges which can cause sales deterioration at some point in their careers. It's essential to understand that sales losing streaks happen. They're a part of every business and every salesperson's career. Top producing salespeople recognize that these situations are temporary and they have the mental and emotional strength to look for creative solutions and the light at the end of the tunnel. The way they control their emotions and attitudes will ultimately determine the length of the losing streak and how quickly they recover or be swallowed by "quicksand."

I've worked with more than one salesperson who got caught up in quicksand. In some cases, it took longer than it should have to break free. In at least one case, an associate really struggled and was ingulfed by "quicksand." It took him years and the threat of divorce to recover because he didn't have the inner strength or mental toughness to pull himself out.

Solutions Come in Many Forms

First, and most importantly, one must absolutely maintain a high level of confidence in his or herself and not dwell on the negative. Additionally, it's imperative to take action of some kind immediately. Procrastination is every sales professionals' worst enemy in good times and, especially, in rough seas. Truly great professionals focus on identifying the cause of the distraction or problem and look for corrections or options as quickly as possible. They put their egos on the shelf and talk with family members, friends, fellow salespeople and even managers. In some cases, even conversations with customers with whom they have great relationships can spark ideas.

Once they identify the cause of the problem, they look to creative solutions for a fix and continue to make sales calls, sales calls and more sales calls. They anticipate potential shortfalls and constantly have their funnel full of new business prospects. They turn on their creative skills which open doors that lead to success. They build on the positive energy and the passion they have for their product or service to work their way out of the "quicksand." Sometimes, they even change sales positions, territories or companies to re-ignite the spark which made them successful in the past. If necessary, they move to a new industry or product to re-energize themselves.

Their strength is in their heads and their hearts...they keep moving forward. Vince Lombardi once said, "The difference between a successful person and others is not a lack of strength, not a lack of knowledge but rather a lack of will." Truly great salespeople use their inner strength and their will to succeed as the springboards to end the spiral and to move forward and up. They take action and avoid dwelling on the negatives.

"The world as we have created it is a process of our thinking. It cannot be changed without changing our thinking." — Albert Einstein

Never Stand Still

It's amazing how many salespeople stay in their comfort zone especially when they've experienced some measure of success. They tend do the same things repeatedly expecting they will continue to grow professionally. Once they feel as though they've achieved a level of success financially, many salespeople tend to get lazy or simply get comfortable and stop attending to the basics.

Early in their careers most salespeople prepare, learn and focus on the details but, as success grows, they tend to take short cuts and assume that yesterday's solutions or ideas will continue to work today and in the future. This can only lead to complacency or plateauing which inhibits growth. Peak performers recognize that sales growth is an ongoing process which includes a balance of tracking market conditions, carefully listening to customers and prospects, experimentation, innovation, taking controlled risks and working hard. They challenge themselves and the status quo constantly to continue to grow professionally. Most importantly, top sales professionals don't rely on the home office to identify the need for change and to alter sales strategy. They are on the front line and are the most qualified individuals to recognize when something isn't working and take the initiative to adjust.

As you focus on improving your skills, strategy and presentation content, it's essential that you constantly prepare for and anticipate inevitable changing conditions. The most successful people in business are those who stay ahead of the wave and aren't simply reacting to things happening around them. You should continuously look for any hint that a change of some kind will improve your position. Are your prospect or customer needs changing? Are they looking for solutions in a different way? Are your competitors changing their tactics or sale strategy leading to changes in customer/prospect perception of your product or brand? Are economic conditions driving changes in prospect or customer attitudes? If we sales professionals are not constantly on the lookout for ways to improve, we're simply standing still and the competition will pass us by.

Identifying the Need for Change

After every prospect or customer meeting, review what worked and think about the prospects' verbal and physical cues which indicated that something you said or presented didn't connect effectively. Every customer or prospect contact represents an opportunity to learn and to sharpen your sales techniques. For example, when you are faced with objections, take the time to evaluate the source. Is there something in your presentation or support material that is confusing or complicated? Are you assuming that the statements you make are always interpreted accurately or the way you intended? Is there a more effective, impactful way to express your sales message?

Be constantly aware that everyone's ideas and personal experiences differ which may cause them to evaluate statements about your product or brand differently than do you. Is the competition planting seeds in prospects' minds which can create conflict and inhibit your sales success? If yes, find answers to these objections and creatively develop the solutions into positive selling points inserted in your sales messages. This action will remove the objection before it becomes an issue in presentations. Pay close attention to and don't be afraid of objections. They can be the most powerful way to determine when change is needed and what needs to be fixed. Use prospect and customer comments and physical cues as measuring tools to determine when changes to the content or the order in your presentations are necessary.

Change the Rules

Strong sales achievers know that playing by the same rules as others breeds conformity and makes it difficult to outpace the competition. They employ unconventional thinking to reshape the rules, create innovative sales strategy and push boundaries. They design unique sales propositions based on feedback from their prospects and customers in order to separate themselves and their products from head-to-head competition with others in the marketplace.

For example, an extremely successful office furniture sales representative once told me that he doesn't sell office furniture...he sells profitability. He explained that there are dozens and dozens of office furniture manufactures which can fill an office space with seating, desks and workstations. While others present their furniture as places to sit and work, he presents the design and quality of his company's furniture as a means to create a comfortable environment, attract high quality employees, enhance productivity and maintain a high level of moral which all lead to greater profitability for the company. After establishing this as a foundation, he follows through with the details and features that support his statements. This process changes the way people think about their needs, what they are actually investing in and his products. This sales strategy establishes him as a partner on a higher or different level than his competitors. It's a perfect example of changing the rules at the expense of competitors.

As you develop and refine your sales strategies, think about what it is you actually sell. How will your product or service impact your prospect? What are the ultimate objectives your prospect might have around which you can build a unique story? How does your competition present their product or service and how can you do so differently? Don't play by everyone else's rules. Redefine the game to best fit your offering and the objectives of your prospects and customers.

Be Flexible in Your Journey

Generally, sales tools provided by the marketing department offer a broad overview of the products or services for your use. But the tools you have should simply be used as a road map for getting from point A to point B. It's up to you and feedback from your prospects to determine which route to take to get to the end result...sales success. It's vital that you concentrate on verbal and physical signs from your prospects in order to determine the direction of your journey. Strong sales achievers are perceptive and flexible during their presentations so that they can take the course which will make sense to their prospects or customers leading to results which pay dividends.

All that said, it's not entirely accurate to assume that one must constantly eliminate old routines or habits especially those which have contributed to success. Great sales professionals don't simply make changes for change sake or because they grow tired of repeating the same thing over and over again. Change should be selective and measured by constant evaluation of prospect responses as well as successes vs failures. We, as sales professionals, need to build on successful past ideas and insert new strategies and tactics when they will improve performance. Top producers continuously compare the information they provide with the results to recognize when changes are needed and what changes will make a difference.

"Creativity requires the freedom to consider unthinkable alternatives, to doubt the cherished practices." - John W. Gardner, Educator, public official and political reformer

Be Creative

Another very important trait which separates top performing salespeople from the rest of the pack is their ability to draw outside the lines or think outside the box – to use a couple of worn out clichés. Whether inherent or learned they are capable of solving problems and enhancing their skills and sales success through finding creative solutions. Throughout this book, we've reviewed ideas and tools like consistent communication, attention getting 2X4's, escaping sales quicksand and dealing with or affecting change. All of these elements, which contribute to elevating sales growth, skills and success, require the ability to think in creative or innovative ways in order to work effectively.

Highly successful professionals know that creative thinking requires an attitude which allows them to break free of the norm and find new ideas. Their knowledge and experience provides a solid base upon which they build new, sometimes unorthodox platforms for greater sales success. And a free-wheeling outlook allows them to explore normal as well as crazy and impractical ideas which are steppingstones to innovative solutions. They're not afraid to break the rules and look to unusual sources to create new opportunities and to overcome objections.

Think Like a Kid

Some years ago, I had the opportunity to attend a seminar on creative problem solving during a builders' conference. After a few introductory words, the speaker started his presentation by asking the question, "Who do you believe are the most creative people on earth?" There were a wide variety of obvious responses including artists, musicians, inventors, architects (it was, after all, a builders' conference), teachers, etc. The answers were all correct on some level but the answer the speaker was really looking for was toddlers. He said, "Think about it...every challenge a toddler faces is new to them so they're forced to find new or creative solutions to every challenge." It's true, toddlers don't have past life experience to draw upon which gets in the way of creative problem solving. As a result, they constantly have to look for new, creative solutions to obstacles they may face. They're not afraid to try numerous options or biased by past experience and they let their imaginations run free to get where they want to go.

We as sales professionals are constantly facing challenges which call for innovative thinking. Although it's useful to rely on past sales successes as a springboard to find answers, yesterday's solutions may not be the best answer for today's obstacles. When looking for a fresh idea, high performance salespeople clear their minds, use past experiences as a starting point and consider wide variety of possible new solutions. Some may be practical and some may be way off the wall but they allow their minds to consider numerous options.

The reality is that the first right answer to a challenge may not always be the best right answer. The most practical solution may be fast and easy to find but it may be the same idea everyone else is using. When you're looking for breakout ideas, take the time to make a list of possible options. Include the obvious answer but let your imagination run free and jot down the ones which seem out of left field. When you're making your list, it pays to forget the old rules, change your point of view or look to other industries or sources for innovative answers. When you think the list is complete, put it aside for a few hours or a day then go back to it to add any additional thoughts which come to mind. Any one of your random ideas may not be the perfect choice but you may find that combining a few unorthodox ideas may provide a unique and unexpected viable answer. Most importantly, let your imagination run free and don't let past experience or "that won't work" naysayers get in the way of finding a creative breakthrough.

Be an Explorer

Innovative ideas can often have their roots outside your immediate area. Look to other industries or businesses for solutions you can adapt to your issues. Be observant and open to ideas all around you. For example, an interior designer once told me that she found inspiration for a custom wallcovering pattern in the marble floor of a cathedral while traveling through Europe. You might find useful ideas which can be adapted to your particular issue in an airport while heading to a flight or during a trip to the museum with your kids or in a TV commercial for a product completely unrelated to your business. The bottom line here is that, when you allow your perceptive skills and your imagination to work full time, you'll often find ideas or answers in unexpected places.

Take Creative Thinking Breaks

Creative solutions can't be forced so another useful practice is to take "thinking breaks" during the day away from the issue at hand. Get away from your office to a local coffee shop or to go to the gym to daydream a little about potential solutions. Consider the problem briefly and let your mind wander almost like meditation. Personally, I find some of my best ideas hit me in the head when I'm mindlessly mowing the lawn. Have a pad of paper and a pen or your smart phone close to jot down any thoughts which can be reviewed and molded when you get back to your desk You'll find this process can prove to be enormously useful and productive.

"Most people do not listen with the intent to understand; they listen with the intent to reply." -Stephen R. Covey, Educator, author, businessman and speaker

Hear...Don't Just Listen

Every salesperson you talk with will tell you they listen to their prospects and customers. The truth is, however, that while most salespeople may be "listening," they often don't really <u>hear</u> what is being said. They tend to be too wrapped up with their own agenda, thinking about the next thing they want to say or accomplish and don't pay enough attention to truly hearing and digesting the comments from their prospect or customer. Unfortunately, failure to hear and take note of these comments can lead to missed opportunities to capture key buying benchmarks which can be used to close the deal. Additionally, prospects and customers can easily recognize when they haven't been heard which leads to disappointment and a lack of respect and confidence in the salesperson.

One example which comes to mind is from a trade show conversation I had with a valuable former customer with whom I had a very strong relationship. She told me she was extremely disappointed with the salesperson who was assigned my old territory after I had moved to a different position. She said that my replacement hadn't done her homework prior to their first meeting, asked very few questions to get to know the customer or the company and sent a follow up email which clearly indicated the she didn't hear or pay attention to anything my former customer had to say about their objectives. My former customer was so disturbed by the meeting and follow up that she wrote to the magazine's publisher to ask if this was really the rep with which she had to work.

An ugly example comes from one of my mentors. He was asked by his partner in a rep firm to attend a few sales meetings with a young, somewhat experienced rep they hired to help guide him along. He had a few years of sales experience in another industry and needed a little mentoring in this market which was new to him. During one meeting in particular, the new rep was cruising through his presentation when the prospect suddenly said, "This is a great solution and the timing is perfect." To my mentor's amazement, the rep nodded, said, "yep" and continued with his pitch. The prospect was ready to buy right then and there! The rep acknowledged the comment but clearly didn't <u>hear</u> the prospect open the door to lock down the sale. They ultimately walked out with the order but, as you can imagine, the young rep got an earful about hearing the customer not just listening.

As mentioned earlier, it's relatively easy for prospects to recognize when they aren't being heard. They become frustrated and insulted which clearly leads to lost opportunities to build a lasting relationship as well as potential sales.

Keys to Hearing Your Prospects

Highly productive sales professionals know that their success is predicated on truly understanding their prospects objectives as thoroughly as possible. They want to hear the prospects' ideas, opinions, needs, buying criteria and any information which will help them demonstrate they offer a perfect solution. They know what they want to accomplish and use an interactive meeting structure to engage the prospect in a two-way conversation through which they capture information vital to their success. They are flexible with their presentation and customize it based on listening and <u>hearing</u>

what their prospect has to say and how they react.

Strong sales producers encourage people to talk about themselves, their company and their needs. They go into every meeting – whether in person, virtual or by phone – prepared with questions designed to help hear how the target thinks and what they want to accomplish. They use the questions to show the prospect they're interested in satisfying their needs, gather vital intelligence and to control the direction and momentum of the conversation. They also employ verbal cues to encourage the prospect/customer to provide more details. Prompts like "I see" or "go on" or "tell me more about that" clearly indicate the salesperson is engaged, is hearing the prospect or customer and sincerely interested in providing a great solution.

Throughout the conversation, highly successful salespeople also take notes. They do so to help remember important prospect comments, areas which need additional probing and to make sure they follow up correctly with any promised material or information. They also periodically refer to the notes during the meeting to probe for additional details about issues important to their prospect or customer. Interestingly, taking notes during a sales meeting has the added benefit of visually demonstrating to the prospect that the salesperson is paying attention and sincerely interested in what the prospect has to say.

Hear with all Your Senses

Top sales produces know that it takes multiple senses to truly understand what their prospects or customers think. Frequently, a prospect may question, not understand or object to a sales statement without verbalizing it. Physical cues like a twitch, change in facial expression or shifting in a chair may indicate that a point made during a sales meeting likely needs to be explained in more detail or explored further. When this happens, it's important to stop the presentation and say something like, "I noticed you seemed uncomfortable with that last point. Do you have a question about what I said or do you need further details about my statement?" This action will help you clarify any questions and show the prospect that you are completely engaged and committed to providing a satisfying solution to their needs.

Clearly, success at sales requires that you learn what will truly satisfy your prospects which can only be achieved by hearing what they have to say about their wants, needs and desires. Passionate salespeople tend to be very excited to tell their story and it takes a great deal of discipline to just shut up and listen to and hear what prospects are thinking. It is this information, after all, which will ultimately lock down the sale.

That said, it's a good idea to practice your listening and hearing techniques. During conversations with family, friends and colleagues consciously make an effort to practice good listening/hearing techniques. Ask questions, probe for more information and be engaged with all your conversations. The more you practice, the more it will become second nature and will carry over into your sales meetings.

Acknowledge that You Heard Them

Lastly, it's essential that you make it very clear that you heard your prospect. Restate the important points or objectives your client mentioned during your meeting in your follow up correspondents. Begin any proposals you send by listing the prospect's stated objectives followed by details about how your product or service will satisfy those objectives. And, when creating a proposal, don't ignore any parameters your client mentions when inviting you to send a proposal. In the event you want to up-sell them, acknowledge the parameters and explain clearly how a larger order will fit their needs more effectively.

"Anyone who stops learning is old, whether at twenty or eighty. Anyone who keeps learning is young. The greatest thing in life is to keep learning." – Henry Ford, Industrialist and founder of the Ford Motor Company

Be a Student and a Teacher

Top sales achievers continuously look for sources to grow professionally, always open to ideas which will help them improve and sharpen their sales skills. While they have a high level of confidence in their ability, great salespeople accept the fact that they can always get better. They are students of their profession as well as people and the industries in which they work. At the same time, highly successful sales professionals find they can also gather creative ideas, learn and grow through mentoring less experienced or struggling sales colleagues.

Be a Student Throughout Your Career

Great sales professionals explore a wide variety of resources ranging from training seminars to books to exchanging ideas with fellow salespeople to learn and improve their skills. Some forward-thinking companies have a formal system in place for salespeople to share ideas and successes. If one salesperson is struggling with tough objections or challenges, you can be sure their associates have hit the same walls as well. Top achievers have enough self-confidence to be open to sharing solutions and/or asking for suggestions. If your sales team has a structure in place for idea exchange, great. If not, don't hesitate to connect with associates you respect and trust for sharing ideas which lead to solutions and increased sales.

Highly successful sales professionals regularly evaluate their performance to learn from past successes and failures. They understand that constantly changing customer and marketplace demands as well as evolving strategies and tactics employed by competitors require constantly fine tuning their own sales strategy, tactics and presentations. Interestingly, a truly valuable feedback or information source can come from conversations with prospects and customers which often provide valuable insights and ideas. This resource assumes, however, that one is perceptive and creative enough to recognizing customer feedback as a source to improve one's sales tactics or strategy. Unfortunately, there are far too many salespeople who are so focused on what they want to say they miss verbal and physical cues offered up by prospects and customers during the conversation. Even more unfortunately, many salespeople aren't capable of translating customer or prospect comments, objections or cues into ways to improve their own sales techniques.

Here's an example of how a customer can positively impact and help fine tune one's sales skill. Early in my career selling magazine advertising, I was calling on the new Marketing Vice President at an office furniture manufacturer. Carlos had worked in marketing at a couple of other firms but it wasn't until joining his current company that he had the responsibility for specifically directing the advertising creative message and sales materials. During our conversation, Carlos said he felt the problem with most advertising and even sales materials is that companies tend focus on features and assume everyone will accurately convert those features to the end benefit which will satisfy the customer's needs. He said his goal was to create sales material and advertising messages which clearly stated the benefit up front and use the features to support how the prospect or customer will reach the benefit. This conversation caused me to rethink and re-organize the structure of my presentations to customers and prospects. I started subsequent conversations with the benefit – investing in advertising with us will grow brand and product awareness leading to greater sales and profits – and used all the supporting features like the circulation, engaging content and readership to show how we would accomplish the end benefit. This change played a huge role in my sales growth and success.

Before your next sales call, take the time to carefully analyze your sales presentation. Are you leading with the what's in it for the customer or prospect? Are you following your benefit statement with a clear presentation of the features which will support the statement? Organizing your presentations and written communications with prospects and customers this way will ensure that you get a high level of the customer or prospects attention throughout your conversation.

Learn from Your Customers' Customers

Another resource for knowledge which can positively affect your success is your customers' customers. For example, if you happen to be selling OEM components and your primary contact is a purchasing manager, it can pay dividends to talk with prototype designers or production managers to learn about their needs. Invite them to lunch or talk with them during trade shows to learn the challenges they face and how your product might impact their performance. Additionally, these types of conversations may even lead to a pull through effect in which they ask the purchasing manager to specifically buy your product or brand. If you were selling nurses' stations to a healthcare system facility manager, talk with their nurses to learn about their workflow and thoughts about what works best for them. Conversations like these will provide you with intelligence you can build into your presentations to everyone who can influence the final buying decision.

Embrace Objections as Learning Tools

Powerfully successful salespeople welcome objections and questions as learning tools. Most often they result from a lack of understanding or misconceptions about their products or services. Frequently, objections may result from misdirection planted in the minds of prospects and customers by competitors. This is most often true when the same objections or questions are raised regularly by prospects and customers.

Top sales performers identify solutions to these to these questions or objections and embed the answers into their presentations as positive selling points. Taking this action blocks the questions before they become issues and erases any doubts even if they are not raised by the prospect or customer. So, learn from and embrace customer or prospect objections and questions, identify solid answers and strategically turn them into positive selling points in your presentations as reasons to buy.

Invest Time in Being a Teacher

Mentoring less experienced or struggling members of your sales team can be enormously gratifying and valuable to you in a couple of ways. Top sales performers find that sharing their experience with young or struggling salespeople can be a valuable way to refresh, in their own minds, the skills on which they've build their success. Old, outdated habits tend to inhibit innovation, growth and progress but reviewing your successes with others can help to reenergize you and remind you of the positive practices which contributed to your sales success in the past.

Secondly, inexperienced or struggling salespeople don't know what they don't know. They don't have preconceived ideas about what works or doesn't work. They ask questions and ask why not. Be patient and open minded because the person you're mentoring may offer perspectives which you may not have considered or perhaps even forgot. They look at the sales process through different, less experienced eyes which can often lead to innovative, creative ideas which may also cause you to ask, "why not." Exchanges like these can help you to reevaluate your routines and sales techniques leading to new, more productive strategies.

"The mind is everything. What you think you become" –
Buddha

A Winning State of Mind

Top performers in every field, especially sales, know that their state of mind has an enormous impact on their success. They balance their intense passion and a tremendously high level of confidence in themselves and their cause to establish and maintain a constant positive attitude. They set high expectations and know their only limitations are in the head and their heart. Through their ever present positive attitude, top performers are able to tap into energy, personal resources and creativity which drives them to excel.

Let Yourself be Great

As you prepare for every component of the sales process, focus your attention on the positive outcome you want to achieve. Know in your mind and your heart that you will succeed. This should be your standard practice applied to every part of your sales effort from face-to-face meetings to phone conversations to written communications and even proposal preparation and writing. Always remember that your success is not determined by what happens to you but by your state of mind and how you react to what happens. A constant positive attitude will cause a chain reaction of affirmative thoughts acting as a catalyst to spark extraordinary results. Conversely, it's essential to avoid even the slightest doubts or negative thoughts throughout the sales process. They will adversely influence your communications, your physical presence and your presentation which, ultimately, impedes reaching your goals.

I witnessed this attitudinal phenomenon first-hand as the National Sale Manager for a residential construction magazine. One of my somewhat less experienced salespeople and I had a meeting with a manufacturer, in his territory, who was investing advertising dollars with our competitors but not with us. When we arrived at the company's office, my salesperson turned to me and said "We aren't going to get him to buy anything. He's just stubborn and doesn't get it." As we walked into the lobby, I could see that the salesperson's attitude had him defeated before we were even greeted by the prospect. His shoulders were slumped and his entire demeanor was negative. His presentation had no energy and the pace of his conversation with the prospect was slow and almost indifferent. Interestingly, I could see that his negative attitude influenced the prospect's mindset as well. He looked bored and disinterested it was clear we weren't going to succeed.

I, being the eternal optimist, wasn't about to let this opportunity slip away. Given the direction we were headed, I took over the conversation, asked questions to get the prospect engaged, raised the level of energy in the meeting, adjusted his perception about the magazine and we ultimately walked out with a request for a proposal. Thankfully, he did eventually invest part of his advertising program with our magazine. Clearly, it's vital to approach every sales situation with a positive frame of mind. You won't always win the day but the right attitude will certainly help you succeed more often than not and avoid defeating yourself right from the start.

See Yourself Succeed

Visualization is another powerful tool used by top sales performers to boost confidence, enhance their positive attitude and increase sales success. When you're faced with what might be a particularly difficult challenge, visualize yourself meeting with the prospect, asking the right questions, learning the way he or she thinks, identifying their needs, hearing their responses and presenting the solutions your product or service offer. Rehearse, in your mind, how you want the conversation to proceed and see yourself succeeding.

One of the best techniques for practicing visualization to enhance success employs past challenging meetings and your successes as a model. Before going into what might be considered a tough meeting, think about past experiences with similar prospects. Create a mental image of the meeting, the questions, the objections, the flow of the meeting and how you resolved issues to reach your goal. Review every detail and then apply your mental picture to the meeting you're about to have. Every meeting will be somewhat different but performing this exercise will help reduce stress and direct the flow of your meeting or conversation in a positive way.

It truly is amazing just how powerful visualization can be in directing the outcome. Numerous studies have been conducted which show the effect visualization can have on performance in sports and in business. For example, a professor conducted an experiment at the University of Chicago in 1996 intended to measure the effects of visualization. Participating students were divided into three groups and asked to prepare for a free-throw shooting experiment. The study started with each student being assigned to a group and asked to shoot free-throws. The percentage of made free-throws was recorded for each.

After this initial step, the first group was asked to practice shooting free-throws for half an hour per day for 30 days. The second group, which was the control group, was told not to practice or play basketball at all for 30 days. The third group was asked to come to the gym every day for 30 days and spend half an hour with their eyes closed visualizing making free-throws. At the end of the 30 day period, the students were asked to return to the gym to take the same number of free-throws they had taken at the beginning of the study. The first group who practiced for 30 minutes each day recorded a 24% improvement in made free throws. The second group which did nothing during the trial period showed no improvement. The third group which visualized making free throws showed a 23% improvement in made free throws. Clearly, visualizing success had a very positive effect on the outcome.

All the ideas and practices outlined in this book will help you grow professionally. But, your state of mind, your attitude and your imagination will, ultimately, determine the level of your success. Always be positive and use visualization as a tool to see yourself succeed. Turning lemons into lemonade is an easy process but one must have the right state of mind to do so.

"Learn from yesterday, live for today, hope for tomorrow. The important thing is not to stop questioning." – Albert Einstein

A Few Final Thoughts

Lester Dundes, one of my most influential mentors, was a demanding boss and brilliant leader. He was a sales superstar for more than 60 years. When Lester talked about sales growth and success, two of the phrases he would often use were "sales isn't rocket science" and "if it were easy, we wouldn't need you." While these may seem to be contradictory phrases, they accurately describe the way top performers view sales as a career. They understand that sales really isn't a complicated process but recognize that challenges do exist and take the initiative to attack them. They build on past successes, learn from past failures and constantly look for ways to improve their skills today and for the future. They constantly question how they can continue to grow professionally.

The fact that you've read this book clearly shows you're committed to your continued sales career growth. Always be passionate, be persistent, be on the lookout for opportunities to change or evolve, be creative, be ever positive and use a few sales 2X4's along the way. Most importantly, don't complicate things and stay out of your own way. Let yourself be great. You'll find that putting the principles highly successful sale professionals employ to work for you will have a huge, positive impact on your success.

Again, good luck and good selling and always shoot for the stars.

www.ingramcontent.com/pod-product-compliance
Lightning Source LLC
Chambersburg PA
CBHW021511210526
45463CB00002B/983